Song of D

Song of Dawn

by

Eloi Leclerc

Translated from the French by
Paul Schwartz and Paul Lachance

FRANCISCAN HERALD PRESS
1434 WEST 51st STREET • CHICAGO, 60609

The *Song of the Dawn* by Eloi Leclerc O.F.M., translated by Paul Schwartz and Paul Lachance from the French *Le Chant des Sources,* Editions Franciscaines, 1972. Copyright © 1977 by Franciscan Herald Press, 1434 West 51st Street, Chicago, Illinois 60609.

Library of Congress Cataloging in Publication Data

Leclerc, Eloi.
  Song of the dawn.

    Translation of Le chant des sources.
    1. Francesco d'Assisi Saint, 1182-1226. Cantico de lo frate sole. I. Title.
  BV489.F74C37513   245   77-22765
  ISBN O-8199-0662-X

June 6, 1977

Nihil Obstat:
  Mark P. Hegener, O.F.M.
  Censor Deputatus

Imprimatur:
  Msgr. Richard A. Rosemeyer, J.C.D.
  Vicar General, Archdiocese of Chicago

Contents

Preface

One might be surprised to realize that profound thoughts are found in the writings of poets rather than philosophers. The reason for this is that poets take advantage of enthusiasm and exploit the power of imagery. Like flint, there are in us the seeds of light. Philosophers evoke them through reason, while poets make them sparkle more brightly by the grace of imagination.

—Descartes, *Cogitationes Privatae*

There is nothing more grotesque than an ass's ear poking out from under a doctor's cap. I once gave a conference in Montreal on the Canticle of Creatures of St. Francis of Assisi, and in the exchange that followed my talk a very distinguished person made the following remark: "The world in which Saint Francis lived had a prescientific mentality. And Francis naturally shared this mentality. This is why he could speak of 'our Sister Water.' But we, raised on a scientific outlook, can no longer speak in this way; we can't even speak of water any longer. We have to say 'H_2O.'"[1]

"You are too reasonable to believe in the sun," said Holderin to the bourgeois writers of his time. In the same way, I could have replied to the above speaker: You are too reasonable to believe in Sister Water.

vii

It is not beside the point to recall that poetry is not a prescientific, prerational language, a primitive and archaic manner of saying things that science has replaced. Science is one language, poetry another. Poetry not only says things differently, poetry says different things. In celebrating the world, the poet speaks the deep dream of man. So even when he seems to be describing nature, he is expressing a secret told to his spirit. All poetry is secret: it journeys toward a promised land, starting out from a lost paradise. It thus opens up the world to the imaginary, to wonder. But, as Aragon points out, "wonder is valuable as a protest against a shattered world, as well as in the creation and transcendence that lead to a better one."

We propose a rereading of Francis of Assisi's Canticle of Brother Sun in this light.

When Francis sings about creation, he evokes not only exterior things but a more vast, more original reality in which the human spirit and material creation encounter one another and discover themselves in a marvelous harmony. "Brother Sun," "Sister Water" —one needs to be a great poet to put these simple words together. And even greater to dare to say: "Sister our mother the Earth." These everyday words, unexpectedly combined in love and dreams, celebrate a homecoming; they express a secret reconciliation where man and the world are reborn into a primal unity.

But we would miss the depth of this experience if we were to forget that the Canticle of Creatures is first of all a great shout of praise lifted toward the Most High, toward the one who is always beyond, whom no one can name. The originality of this canticle can be found in the fact that this shout toward the transcendent, which is affirmed so neatly in the first stanza and which seems bound to tear man loose from earth, suddenly opens onto fraternal and won-

derous communion with all creatures. The shout toward
highest heaven here passes through this communion.
This is the first point we have tried to bring a light.

A second point also should receive our attention.
This fraternal communion with creatures and the
enthusiastic celebration it expresses are also the language of man's opening to his whole being. Man cannot fraternize truly and deeply with the cosmic elements without reconciling himself to all that these
elements symbolize, that is to say, with his inner
"archaeology," with all the obscure forces that com-
prise his primal being. In his Canticle of the Sun,
Francis discovers the luminous meaning of creation.
But he does so by starting from an interior experience
that is a new genesis, a new creation. "He seemed
like a new man, a man of the age to come," his
first biographer says of him.[1] It was in becoming this
new man that Francis perceived the meaning of creation. His canticle is not only a stirring tribute to
the Creator, it is also the celebration of an inner
becoming. He sings the new creation in the very
heart of man.

Francis of Assisi wrote no learned theses. But when
he wanted to tell us his vision of things, this brother
of the troubadours started singing. He sang about all
creatures. And in this song he gave us the depths of
his soul and the secret of his new birth. His canticle
is the confession of a man in whom the basic forces
of life have recovered the transparency of the primal
sources and the brilliance of a sunburst.

The Birth of a Song

It is night; here the voice of all living waters is raised. And my
soul, too, is a living spring.

—Nietzsche

The Canticle of the Sun is a song about light. But
this song emerged from the darkest night.

Francis was not yet forty-five years old, but fatigue,
deprivation, and long vigils had ruined his health.
He had less than two years to live. On the solitary
heights of Alverna, he had just received the signs of
the Passion of Christ in his flesh. He had become what
he had never stopped contemplating: someone pierced
through. In great pain, on the back of a donkey, he
came down from the mountain and set off on the road
to Assisi. But the ardent spirit that was guiding him
moved him to spread the gospel wherever he went.

Shortly after his return to the Portiuncula, he had
himself taken to San Damiano, where Clare and her

sisters lived. A health problem turned this visit into
a forced stay of several months. Ever since his return
from the Middle East, Francis had suffered from a
running eye. This ailment suddenly grew worse and
brought on an acute crisis. Francis practically lost his
sight. Violent headaches tormented him. It was impossible to return to the Portiuncula. Sister Clare
installed the sick man and his companions in a small
house adjoining the cloister. And to protect Francis'
eyes from bright daylight she set up an alcove with
straw matting.

For more than fifty days Francis dwelled in this
dark little cell, unable to bear the least glimmer of
sunlight in the day or the least flicker of fire in the
night. He suffered so much from his eyes that he
could neither rest nor sleep. And mice, scurrying
around the room—even running over his body—gave
him not a moment's rest.

Physical suffering was joined by other cares. Francis thought of the multitude of brothers the Lord had
given him and of the mission that was theirs. He had
never felt so poor and used up. And during those
long days of inaction he saw his whole life unfold-
ing before him: everything the Lord had done for
him and how he had tried to respond.

Twenty-five years earlier, in this very place, in the
church of San Damiano, which was no more than a
small, abandoned, and delapidated chapel, Francis
had heard Christ's call: "Go, repair my house, which,
as you see, is falling into ruin." In his simplicity and
with his innate sense of the specific and down to earth,
he became a mason on the spot. With his hands he
restored not only San Damiano but two other little
churches in the countryside of Assisi.

Then one day, while attending a Eucharist in one
of the little chapels that had been brought back into
use through his care, he heard the gospel text con-

cerning the sending of the disciples on mission: "Go
. . . Proclaim on the road that the reign of heaven
is near. . . . Take neither gold nor silver, nor a sack
for the road, nor two tunics, nor sandals, nor staff."
Francis' spirit was flooded by a real illumination. Repairing the house of God was not, as he had thought,
resetting stone upon stone. It meant coming back to
the mission passages of the gospel, rediscovering the
condition of the disciples sent forth by the master.
"This is what I have been looking for, this is what I
have been burning to accomplish from the depths of
my heart!" he cried out at that instant. And he im-
mediately left the solitude in which he had been
living since his conversion and set off toward other
men and women, just as Christ had asked him: without goods, without supplies, without power. Yes, that
was really it; that was how to repair the Church that
was falling into ruins.

Then the Lord gave him brothers. With them,
Francis set about trying to build real fraternities modeled on the gospel. Fraternities of poor men, holding
no property; powerless, without any kind of defense;
fraternities truly different from the rich abbeys of
that era. The friars made no pretense of playing any
role in society; they simply wanted to announce the
"good news" to all. The fraternities multiplied; and
a gentle breath of tenderness swept over that century
of fire and iron.

Christendom did not turn away from its policy of
violence, especially where Islam was concerned. Its
preoccupation was not mission but the crusade. A
harsh crusade in the name of the truly gentle Lord!
So Francis left for the Orient. Not as a crusader, but
as a man of peace, with empty hands, to proclaim to
the sultan "the coming of tenderness." Wasn't this
also repairing the Church of Christ?

But Francis did not convert the sultan. Nor did he

convert the Crusaders, who poured over the city of Damietta and sacked it with the savage cruelty of wild beasts. Francis returned weakened, sick, and almost blind. Moreover, he had to hasten his return, for dissenion had broken out between the brothers. The vicars general to whom Francis had confided the governing of his order during his absence had allowed themselves to add new prescriptions to the friars' rule of life. These prescriptions, which tended to bring the brothers' life into conformity with traditional monasticism, troubled the spirits of those who remained very attached to the primitive ideal of Francis. On the other hand, the number of brothers had grown considerably. A need for some organization was felt. There were many clerics among the newcomers—men of some learning. Not everyone shared the simplicity of the first friars. Even a certain wish for prestige and power arose among a few of the brothers—an outright negation of what Francis had wanted. Under such circumstances, everything could be questioned from one day to the next.

In the shadows of his cell, Francis thought over these events for long days and long nights. He heard once again, from across the reaches of his memory, the Lord's call: "Francis, go repair my house, which is falling into ruin." Measured against this call, everything he had undertaken until now seemed so little, like a joke or even a dead end. And Francis asked himself what the Lord wanted from him now. Speaking to his companions, he said: "Up until now we have done nothing. Let's start to do something."

"Do something"! But what? There was no longer any question of running across mountains and valleys to proclaim the "good news." He was immobilized, his eyes a constant torture, his body a ruin. Condemned to inaction and silence. And as the days passed, the more Francis seemed to become shrouded in darkness.

Was this repairing the house of God?

Sister Clare kept watch in the nearby cloister. She who had followed Francis' path from the beginning and who gladly referred to herself as "his little plant" understood many things. She knew that after this long voyage to the end of night, brightness would return to Francis' soul. And then he would speak of the really important things. Her role was to pray and to wait in silence.

Then one night, full of insomnia and suffering, Francis was at the end of his strength and on the verge of despair. He begged God to pity him. All at once he heard a voice inside: "Francis, rejoice as if you were already in my kingdom." And at the same time a very gentle light entered his soul: the light of the kingdom at hand. And this light made him see all things new. It was like Easter morning. At that moment the whole world seemed touched by the glory of God. The kingdom had already begun, here and now, in pure splendor.

This was no time to turn in on oneself, to moan or look back or dream of other things. This was the time to celebrate and sing. "Rejoice"! This was what the Lord wanted from him now. Rejoice with all of creation. "Your business is joy, the joy of things all together."[1] There was nothing more important for the future of the Church and the world. This, too, was repairing the house of God!

And so an immense surge of praise lifted up Francis' spirit, waking in him dormant reserves of enthusiasm and the wondrous gaze of a child. And this praise held the splendor of the sun, the brilliance of the stars, the wings of the wind, the murmuring of water, the impetuosity of fire, and the humility of the earth. A great sun rose in Francis' soul. Day broke over Assisi. It was a morning marvelous with light. Francis called his companions. He was radiant. He sat up, concentrated a moment, and started to sing:

> Most High, all powerful, good Lord,
> to you all praise, glory and honor
> and all blessing;
> to you alone, Most High, they belong,
> and no man is worthy of naming you.
>
> Praised be you, my Lord,
> with all your creatures,
> especially Milord Brother Sun,
> who brings day, and by whom you enlighten us:
> he is beautiful, he shines with great splendor;
> of you, Most High, he is the symbol.
>
> Praised be you, my Lord,
> for Sister Moon and the Stars:
> in the heavens you formed them,
> clear, precious, and beautiful.
>
> Praised be you, my Lord, for Brother Wind
> and for the air and for the clouds,
> for the azure calm and all climes
> by which you give life to your creatures.
>
> Praised be you, my Lord, for Sister Water,
> who is very useful and humble,
> precious and chaste.
>
> Praised be you, my Lord, for Brother Fire,
> by whom you enlighten the night:
> he is beautiful and joyous,
> indomitable and strong.
>
> Praised be you, my Lord,
> for Sister our mother the Earth
> who nourishes us and bears us,
> and produces all kinds of fruits,
> with the speckled flowers and the herbs.

This man, who bore the wounds of Christ in his flesh, sang about the fraternity of sun, stars, wind, water, fire, and earth. Never had such a meeting been produced between the dark night of deprivation and the splendor of the world, between the cross and the sun.

This song, which celebrates the wedding of heaven and earth, was truly the song of the new man touched by the glory of God. It was the song of man reconciled and saved.

This poem was not a pure improvisation. Francis had borne it within him for some time. To tell the truth, he had been humming it all his life. One finds hints of it in the everyday stuff of his life. But in its finished form, this song sprang forth at the end of a long spiritual itinerary—so much so that it was one with Francis' whole life, with the deep growth of his being. And this final springing forth was one of those creative moments when one's being, gathering all its vital forces and all its history in one simple emotion, suddenly gives birth to a new language that expresses it totally.

2
A Hymn to Transcendence

Most High, all powerful, good Lord,
to you praise, glory, honor and
all blessing;
to you alone, *Most High,* they belong,
and no man is worthy of naming you.

The Canticle of Brother Sun opens with a great burst of praise. The first words, "Most High," send the song soaring toward the heights. Taken up a second time in the first stanza in an absolute way, they forcefully indicate the sole aim of all praise. This image of the Most High expresses transcendence. It will return four times throughout the canticle. Toward it all Francis' energies of praise are raised.

Such an outburst translates the orientation of a life. "Reaching out to you, Most High", is the vow Francis formulates at the end of his *Letter to a Chapter.* All his life breathed the transcendent reality of God. Even on a physical plane, his being was lifted up by this vertical movement of the soul. No wonder we sometimes see him clambering up mountainsides to give himself over to contemplation of the Only.

This cry toward highest heaven, toward the Most High, expresses a movement of self-transcendence. Man is not a being who exists folded in on itself, enclosed once and for all within set limits. "Man," wrote Pascal, "is made for infinity." He only really exists in the movement that opens him to infinite grandeur. There only does he breathe his native air: he discovers himself in the image of God. Man aspiring to the Most High is a being touched by transcendence.

This impulse can be lived in different ways. It can be lived in an effort at self-mastery, as a retrieval of our ultimate depth, and no more. The infinitude to which man is destined is thus sought in a possessive and Promethean way, as a good that is ours by right. To be God without God is the old dream of man, his permanent temptation from the start.

With Francis, this impulse toward the Most High is lived in a wholly different way. What forcefully marks the first stanza of his canticle is a movement of disappropriation:

> . . . to you praise, glory, honor and all benediction;
> to you, Most High, they belong.

This impulse toward the Most High is purified of every possessive motive. Throughout his life Francis did not cease to react against this desire to appropriate, which is in each man and woman and secretly corrupts his or her aspiration to the divine. This was the profound meaning of his poverty: the renunciation of appropriating to himself what belongs to God, or even God himself. No wonder he comes back to this idea so many times in his writings: we should not lay claim to the good we do, nor even to the desire for good that is within us, but should give all honor to him who is the source of all good.[1]

At the end of his life, nothing remained in Francis but a very pure desire for God. In his canticle his shout of praise toward the Most High joins with the greatest inner poverty. Here there is no turning in on the self, no complacency, no consideration of a personal nature. Self-love, cares, regrets—all are swept away. There is room for nothing but adoration. Francis recognizes the sovereignty of God. And his joy is immense to know that God alone is God.

This recognition of the transcendence of God has nothing crushing about it. It is fulfilled, on the contrary, in a feeling overflowing with gratitude. It is essentially thanksgiving. This is because the Most High is not only the All Powerful; he is also the "good Lord." More precisely, he is all power for good. Adoration, for Francis as for the whole Christian mystical tradition, is not merely bowing before an All Powerful, which dominates us; it is also recognizing that this All Powerful is infinetely holy and good, that it is a pure and sovereign will for the good. The adoring man says not only "God is" but also "he is worthy of being God, worthy of being the All Powerful." In the *Praises,* which he wrote and which he recited at every canonical hour, day and night, Francis expressed his adoration with this doxology, which he freely borrowed from the Apocalypse: "You are worthy, Lord, our Father, to receive honor, praise and glory, and to be proclaimed blessed."

Nietzsche wrote: "Let us be done with the concept of God the supreme goodness; it is unworthy of a God. Let us be done even with the supreme wisdom; the vanity of the philosophers imagined this absurdity, a God who would be a monster of wisdom. . . . No! God is the *supreme power:* that is enough!" If God were, effectively, nothing but the All Powerful, we

would undoubtedly be truly obliged to crush ourselves before him, but we would not be able to give
him the free assent of our person. "Let us make the
absurd supposition for a moment," wrote Romano
Guardini, "that God, infinite reality and limitless
power, is only blind and brutal force and nothing
else; in this case, I must not bow down inwardly
before him. He would be able to suppress my life;
yet my person should refuse him adoration. For me
to adore him, he needs to be not only powerful,
but worthy of being so."

For Francis of Assisi, there was no hesitation: God
is truly worthy of being God. And his whole person
experienced a great calm at this single thought. The
transcendence Francis contemplated is not, in fact, a
distant reality shut in on itself. It manifests itself to
us in the mystery of the Incarnation, in the humanity
of the Son of God. The transcendence of God is to
be sought nowhere else; it cannot be dissociated from
this mystery of humility and love. And this is why
God is truly worthy of being God: "Worthy is the
Lamb that was slain," wrote Francis, "to receive force
and divinity, wisdom, power, honor and glory, and to
be proclaimed blessed."[2]

Francis's adoration holds nothing back. It is unending wonder. In the humility of the Son of God,
Francis discovers the hidden splendor of the Most
High, the splendor of a love that, with no merit
on our side, reaches us and joins us in the depths of
our distress. This "wondered" gaze on God releases
him from himself and gives him over to praise.

But Francis is aware of the limits of his praise. The
first stanza of his canticle ends with this verse: "and
no man is worthy of naming you." God is not only
he to whom all praise is directed, he is above all
praise. Even in the light of revelation, man can
fashion no idea worthy of him. God is always the

Mysterious. Even though he is with us, he is still beyond. He is always beyond the idea we make of him for ourselves.

The thought expressed in this last verse is already apparent in the First Rule: "All of us, indigents and sinners, we are not worthy of naming you."[3] We should give the act of naming its biblical significance here for, in the Bible a name expresses a person or thing in its profound calling. The act of naming is thus a grasp of being, a taking possession of being by the spirit. So in Genesis, man, after being created by God, is invited to name every animal in creation and to affirm in that very act his mastery over all of them.[4] But when Jacob asks the name of the unknown opponent whom he has been wrestling all night long, he heard him say: "Why are you asking me my name?"[5] Yet Jacob was recognized by his adversary as "stronger than God." But the God who lets himself be conquered remains God. He jealously guards his mystery, simply because he is God, because he is the Unique. Around God, there is an unfathomable glory.

"The Most High," writes Eliade, "is a dimension inaccessible to man as such." And this is what Francis recognized. The God he proposes to praise in his Canticle of Creatures is not the world-soul, nor even the ultimate depth of man. It is the God who is unspeakably raised over all that is, even over all that can be thought. It is the God whose elevation cannot be expressed by the creature.

We cannot rush over this last verse of the first stanza; to do so would be extremely superficial. It would also be a misunderstanding of the real dimension of the religious universe of Francis of Assisi. We will never be able to express how much this universe soars toward the transcendent. The different prayers the *Poverello* left us are all a celebration, as is this first stanza of his canticle, of the transcendence of God.

Such a celebration is part of the most pure tradition of the great mystics. It is worth recalling the hymn of Gregory of Nazienzen:

> O you, the beyond of all,
> how should we call you by another name . . .
> You, the only one we cannot name.

At the end of the first stanza of the Canticle of Brother Sun we would hardly be surprised to see Francis' song fold itself in silence. The saint's gaze seems to have broken away from earth to lose itself entirely in the direction of the Most High.

3

Cosmic Fraternity

The Canticle of Creatures is above all a great outburst of praise turned toward the Most High. But this impulse, which at first sight seems to lift many away from earth, functions in this instance through a fraternal communion with all creatures: "Praised be you, my Lord, with all your creatures." Here is the originality of this canticle. In order to praise God, Francis did not feel the need to belittle his creatures. Not through proclaiming the insignificance of things and seeking ways to avoid them does he go toward God. The very opposite is true: he takes himself toward the Most High by unifying himself with all of creation on a very profound level and by standing in wonder before all things. His praise of the Most High is also a praise of creatures. The original character of Francis of Assisi's message, writes Louis Lavelle, "is to be the highest affirmation that can be made of the value of the person and of life such as we have received them from the very hands of God."

This originality is all the more striking when we realize that a strong current of spirituality directed the most zealous spirits of that day in a completely opposite direction. We know the repercussions of the Catharist doctrine in the Christianity of the Middle Ages. In the name of a purified faith, this doctrine set God and the material creation in opposition. The world of matter was considered the kingdom of the spirit of evil: a realm of darkness that had to be left behind in order to enter into the light of the spirit of God. Francis of Assisi obeyed a wholly different inspiration. At the very heart of material realities he discovered a path of light toward the Most High.

In doing so, Francis placed himself in the biblical tradition, that of the Psalms and the prophets who praised God in all his works. "Just as, formerly," wrote Thomas of Celano, "the three young men in the furnace invited all the elements to praise and glorify the creator of the universe, so Francis, full of the spirit of God, continually glorified, praised, and blessed the creator and master of all things for all the elements and all creatures."[1]

But Francis brings a really original and personal note to biblical inspiration. He is not content only with praising God for his creatures, he fraternizes with them all. And this is new. What is most striking in all of his canticle, in fact, is that each cosmic element is called brother or sister. Francis knew no sun, no wind, no water, no fire, etc., but "Brother Sun," "Brother Wind," "Sister Water," "Brother Fire." This was no simple, allegorical way of speaking on his part. He really felt in everyday life a brotherhood with the most material creatures. A new kind of sensitivity saw the light of day here.

This cosmic fraternity had deep roots in Francis. It connected, first of all, with his very living faith in the universal fatherhood of God. "Having climbed to the first Origin of all things," wrote St. Bonaventure, "Francis conceived an overflowing friendship for them, and called even the most humble creatures 'brother' and 'sister,' for he knew that he and they proceeded from one and the same principle."[2] This theological and—so to speak—metaphysical vision is at the very heart of the cosmic fraternity of Francis. Yves Congar correctly states that "it was in the strongest theological sense of the word, and not only in function of a pleasant poetry, that Francis spoke of birds, fire, the sun, . . . of death itself as his brother and sisters."

Nonetheless, this profound intuition of his was not reduced to a purely intellectual vision. In truth, it is not primarily that. Enthusiasm and creative lyricism spring with difficulty from a mere idea. The cosmic fraternity of Francis is inseparable from an experience of sympathy and affective participation with all that lives and all that is. It is first of all felt at this level. Francis had an exceptional gift for sympathy. Thomas of Celano and St. Bonaventure recognized this: "The wholly natural feelings of his heart were already enough to make him fraternal with every creature."[3] This remark is important. Without this affective investment in one's relationship to things and creatures, the most beautiful declarations of fraternity ring false.

Nevertheless, it would be wrong to reduce this affective experience to a question of pure sentimentality. What we have here is much deeper and more vast. The emotion that moved Francis' whole being in the presence of the least creature is itself a perception of value. Francis directly and intensely perceived the value of all life and all being as manifestations of creative love. It was at this depth that the current between him and creation was established. In his sympathy for creatures he vibrated with them and opened himself to the primal breath of life and being. From this came his attitude of respect and veneration before all that is. From this, too, came the penetrating gaze that allowed him to discover the original vitality at the heart of every being. Thomas of Celano wrote: "He called all creatures brother or sister; and in an extraordinary way unknown to others, thanks to the perspicacity of his heart, he knew how to penetrate to the utter most intimacy of each creature."[4]

What Bergson says of mystical love is fully verified here: "It is neither sensible nor rational. It is the one and the other implicitly, and it is effectively much more. For such a love is at the very root of sensibility and reason, as of all other things. Coinciding with the love of God for his creation, the love that made everything, it gives to him who knows how to ask the secret of creation. It is metaphysical much more than moral. . . . Its direction is that of life's elan; it is this élan itself , integrally communicated to some privileged men." It was in sympathy with this creative élan that Francis fraternized deeply with all creatures.

This fraternal presence to the world risks seeming hardly realistic today. Many people will see it as a fanciful dream. Our behavior before natural realities is in fact marked by our obedience to a wholly different inspiration. Industrial civilization is built entirely on the idea that man is "the master and possessor of nature"; it rests on a will to power in the face of nature. Man does not cease to increase his power over nature by inventing means of action that are continually more perfect and more efficient. In the face of such power, nature is nothing but a mass of objects to be dominated and exploited, or a reservoir of energies to be conquered and depleted. Man in the industrial age has broken away from nature; he has deliberately set himself above it. Between him and nature there is now a sovereign technique that leaves no place for any communion whatever, but only the will to dominate. Strengthened by his power, man submits nature in all its domains to a real shock treatment in order to have it produce its maximum.

But today we are discovering the limits of such an attitude. Ecologists the world over are anxiously asking themselves what will become of the human race if it continues to devote itself to this invasion and pillaging of nature. For man is destroying his natural environment. Water and air are becoming increasingly polluted, lands are laid waste, plant and animal species are on their way to extinction; a whole balance has been upset. On the other hand, as soon as nature is considered only as an instrument of power, it becomes a pawn in a struggle between men for power. In such a way our human relationships are falsified and profoundly altered as a consequence of our relation to nature, considered all together under the sign of the will to possession and power. To refuse fraternity with nature is also, to be sure, to render oneself incapable of fraternity between men.

It is for this reason that an attitude like St. Francis' toward the realities of nature should not be taken lightly. It merits a close look. Perhaps now, more than ever, we need to rediscover the spirit of this cosmic fraternity.

But let us first clear the air of a misunderstanding. To be fraternal with lesser creatures in no way means to renounce their use or to renounce putting them at the service of human needs. Francis recognized the utility of things: they are fraternal in their very utility. Brother Sun gives us light: "he brings the day." Brother Wind, with his powerful breath, reinvigorates all living creatures. Sister Water is explicitly sung about as "useful." Brother Fire brightens our night. And Sister our mother the Earth nourishes us by producing all kinds of fruits. There is thus no room for opposing fraternity with creatures to their utilization by man.

The power that man has gained over nature, thanks to the progress of science and its techniques, can even make the cosmic elements more fraternal by freeing them from everything blind or destructive in them.

What, then, does fraternity with all creatures mean in a positive sense? It is something that involves the whole of man, and it is not easy. It presupposes a real conversion of one's gaze and one's heart.

The temptation of all power is violence. Man violates nature when, flushed with the strength of his power over it, he submits it to his desire for profit. He violates it even further when he uses this same power to unleash his will to power against nature. And that can be taken very far. Drunk with his conquests, man today would like to take the place of the All Powerful, to appropriate creative power to himself, to refashion the world in his own way, and finally to become the master of life and his own creation. The Promethean dream is at the heart of the conquest of the world. And the will to power grows to become a will to self-creation. This project is not pursued without aggression and violence against everything that links us to nature, against everything that makes us dependent beings linked to a reality and a history that reach beyond us.

This project is fundamentally a revolt against our creaturely condition and therefore against the very transcendence of God. The rejection of our roots is always the defiance of transcendence.

The man who is fraternal with creatures renounces this revolt. He recognizes himself as a creature and reintegrates the great family of creatures. To welcome the most humble fraternal elements as brothers and sisters is to admit that direct family ties exist between them and oneself, ties that lead back to a common and transcendent source.

Before the Most, whom ''no man is worthy of naming," Francis counts himself among creatures "with great humility." In doing so, he recognizes that only God is God and is worthy of being so. Fraternal communion with creatures is a part of his approach to adoration.

But in so acting, Francis is truly born to the world and to himself. Nothing can prevent his instincts of sympathy and benevolence from developing fully. No superiority complex can inhibit them. Nothing remains of man, shut up in his aggressivity on the one hand, or of an alien and hostile universe on the other. There is only the work of God that is profoundly one. Francis discovers himself at the heart of a unity of creation. And the current of sympathy that links him to other beings joins him to the creative love himself. "In each creature, as in so many rivulets," wrote St. Bonaventure, "he perceived with an extraordinary piety the unique springing forth of the goodness of God."[5] Not only did he perceive this original goodness, he participated in it. From this fraternal man, the friend of all creatures, shone forth a strength and a warmth that entered into things and made them more rich, more luminous, and more pleasant. "There undoubtedly never was a man who offered to all more perfectly this total presence and this whole gift of self which are nothing more than the expression of the presence and the gift which God makes of himself at every instant and to every individual."[6]

In the light of an existence like that of Francis of Assisi, it is clear that it is not by violating and enslaving nature that man can ameliorate the quality of his existence, but by cooperating with the work of creation in which every living thing participates. In the drunkeness of his new power, the man of industrial society has behaved like a despot toward nature. For a long time now, he has imagined himself Prometheus. Perhaps he is now beginning to realize that his true strength lies in perceiving himself as a responsible creature. Responsible and fraternal.

This cosmic fraternity necessarily passes through the humble recognition of our creaturely condition. It does not work without a profound self-dispossession that the Canticle of Creatures echoes by celebrating the most humble elements as brothers and sisters, including "our mother the Earth."

By remaining under the protection of the earth, with all that lives, Francis lifts himself toward the Most High. His song, in its burst of brilliant azure, retains the hue of its first furrow.

4

Wonder

Being fraternal with creatures means being willing
to take one's place with them and rediscovering one's
links to them. This can't be done simply with will
power. Only wonder can pull man out of his splendid isolation. It is the incantation of poetry that releases him from self-sufficiency and brings him to birth
in the world.

Francis of Assisi is the man of wonder. He possessed
an exceptional capacity to be amazed. For him,
things were not simply a pretext for praising God.
He found them beautiful, very beautiful. And this
beauty fascinated him. The adjective "beautiful" appears three times in his canticle. Remarkably, each
time it is attributed to a luminous element: the sun,
the stars, and fire. Light had the capacity to spark a
feast in his soul. Thomas of Celano wrote: "Contemplating the sun, the moon, the firmament and all the
stars, he felt an ineffable joy rise in his heart."[1] But
his wonder reached out to all creatures: "What an

opening of his entire soul when he considered the
beauty of things, Francis no longer belonged to himself. Being among creatures was a real splendor for
him. "We who lived with him," wrote his first companions, "have seen him rejoice interiorly and ex-
teriorly over all creatures, to such a point that in
touching them or seeing them his spirit seemed not
on earth, but in heaven." [3]

We would like to analyze Francis' capacity for wonder and see how it is a part of his religious experience of the world.

We have pointed out the natural gifts of sympathy
and benevolence at the root of Francis' fraternal
love for creatures. Likewise, at the base of his capacity for wonder is the sensitivity of the artist and the
poet. From his youth, Francis was sensitive to the
beauty of nature. It is significant that the first time
he went outdoors, following his illness on his return
from captivity in Perugia, he went out to contemplate the surrounding countryside: he wanted to rediscover the enchantment of light, color, and contour.
And yet this time there was no enchantment to be
found. But, even so, Francis' disappointment attests
to a friendship already established.

This sensitivity to the beauty of the world deepened
and matured with experience, but it always exhibited
a characteristic that had been present from its first
awakening: a particular candor before things. The
wondered regard of Francis was a naïve regard. He
ignored the whole mythological apparatus the ancients
had used to explain the elements of nature. He also
ignored the learned allegories of the clerics. His regard
went to the thing itself, in its immediate and tangible
reality. The stars and flowers Francis contemplated were
real stars and flowers. Stars and flowers unburdened
of their mythic dressing and restored to their native
truth and their primal freshness. Stars and flowers

worthy of being looked at for themselves. The tangible world thus recovers a value in itself.

Moreover, all the things Francis celebrated he knew in a very direct and realistic way. They were the unpolished company of his life as a pauper. Ever since he began to restore the little churches in the countryside of Assisi after his conversion, he lived down to earth, with stone, water, sun, and wind. And when he traveled on the roads of Italy in all kinds of weather or when he retired to a mountain to stay in a comfortless hermitage, he was in permanent contact with the untamed reality of things. And it was precisely this truly simple and unpolished reality that threw him into wonder. In the *Fioretti* is a story that illustrates this perfectly. Brother Francis and Brother Masseo had been begging their meal in a village; having finished their task, they went to eat in a solitary place, where there was a beautiful spring and, next to it, a great, beautiful rock shaped like a table. They placed their bits of bread on the rock. Then Francis, looking at the spring, the table of rock, and the bread, exclaimed: "Brother Masseo, we are not worthy of such treasure!" As he repeated this several times, Brother Masseo could not help asking, "Father, how can you speak of treasure where there is so much poverty and when so much is lacking? There is no cloth, no knife, no cutting board, no bowl, no house, no table . . . " And Francis answered him: "That is exactly what I see as a great treasure — there is nothing here which has been prepared by human industriousness. Everything is God's gift: the begged bread, the beautiful rock table and the clear water of the spring."[4]

The beauty of things, such as Francis discovered it, is not a surface arrangement, a quaint prettiness or mere decoration. Things are there beneath his gaze in their original nakedness, like an epiphany of being. Beauty is this secret splendor radiated by the things themselves. It is but one with the miracle of existence.

This esthetic of poverty and humility rejoins the truth of created things. The things Francis celebrates in his canticle are marked by a disconcerting simplicity. No artifice deforms them. But they all shine. They are luminous on the strength of their simplicity. The humblest as well as the greatest. Sister Water, so close to the soil, shines with the same brilliance as the stars in the heavens. Each one sheds light on the mystery of being. And this mystery is light itself: this is what the song proclaims.

Only the dispossessed and transparent soul has the purity that allows it to see this splendor and to recognize therein the allure and the symbol of the invisible beauty of the Creator. "Francis," wrote Thomas of Celano, "knew how to contemplate the All-Beautiful in one beautiful thing."[5] In the torrent, he saw the source.

We cannot separate the wondered regard of Francis from his deep and interior life. Like the troubadours of his age, to whom he compared himself, he celebrated nature in terms of the love that fired his heart. His song of the world is intimately linked to his contemplation of Christ. "Very often while on a trip, because he was meditating upon and singing of Jesus," wrote Celano, "he forgot about his walk and invited all the elements to praise Jesus with him."[6] We cannot call too much attention to the fact that the man who sang the Canticle of the Sun is the stigmatized man of Alverna who carried in his whole being the burning image of incarnate love.

At the beginning of the troubadours' songs there is always a springtime that is starting to flower. Spring, resplendent with the blossoming of orchards and filled with the songs of birds, is the image of the poet's heart. He loves, and his heart is transfigured by this love. And this intimate transfiguration brings him to see new things; it makes him participate, through wonder, in the metamorphosis of the world.

What human love worked in the troubadours, divine love worked in Francis, but with much more truth and depth. The luminous and fraternal world be contemplated and sang about, he discovered by starting from what he experienced in himself, in his intimate relation with Christ. This was the experience of a new creation. The great creative love to which Francis opened himself made a new man of him, a man of the world to come. And the wondered regard that he trained on the world is that of a man who discovers all things in a pascal light. It is a prophetic and creative regard. Thomas of Celano wrote with much insight: "The Beauty that is at the source of all things and which one day will be all in all things already in this life appeared all in all things to the eyes of the saint."[7] Is not all creation already reconciled and fraternally reunited in the risen Christ?

It is in this light that these expressions of the canticle have all their meaning: Brother Sun, Sister Moon, Brother Wind, Sister Water, Brother Fire. . . . These images, which establish a direct kinship between man and the world, are meant to express reality in its wholeness and its unity. They erase all borders. They recover a plenitude of being that goes beyond every concept. These images constitute a move beyond any kind of split or rupture at the heart of being. They celebrate unity: the unity of man and nature, of spirit and life, of freedom and necessity. They sing of a return to the source of being, to the infancy of the world.

Francis did not seek this unity behind him, in the past. For him, it did not so much evoke a lost paradise as it expressed the very meaning of the world's becoming in Christ. The fraternal and wondered vision of Francis is not some vision of a primal state of nature to which we can either return or abandon ourselves but, rather, a vision of a world working for reconciliation in which the primacy of conciliation over rupture is already affirmed due to the deed accomplished by Christ. The universal fraternity of Francis is less a nostalgic memory of some first innocence than an ardent hope of forgiveness and renewal. Redemption, with its power of resurrection, here brightens creation. The sun, resplendent in Francis' song, is that of Easter morning. "Rejoice as if you were already in my kingdom," Christ told him.

Every poetic regard is a quest for the promised land. But most often the poet does not enter the promised land. He sees it from afar, like Moses. It is only through intention and in a symbolic way that his song restores the integrity of the world. "These woods are lovely, dark and deep / But I have promises to keep / And miles to go before I sleep / And miles to go before I sleep."[8]

But the poet can also be a man of faith; he can be a saint. Then for us he is like one of the men who were sent out to reconnoiter the Promised Land and who came back loaded with fruit, saying: "It's a wondrous country. Look at it; it's very near, under the Eveningstar."

5

The Depth Dimension

We know the important place that dreams, images, and symbols held in the life of St. Francis of Assisi, starting with the first reveries that helped to clarify his vocation and including the appearance of the Canticle of Creatures. In an earlier volume,[1] devoted to this canticle, we tried to show that this oneric aspect of the poetic and religious personality of the saint can reveal the inner scope of his itinerary toward God. We have no intention of returning to that analysis in detail, but simply want to call the reader's attention to this depth dimension of the canticle.

The creatures Francis celebrates are not only observed, they are also dreamed — discreetly, perhaps, but in a manner nonetheless real and profound. Thus "Milord Brother Sun" is not merely a simple physical phenomenon, he is a living thing; he not only gladdens the eye, he also speaks to the soul; he brings about an immense joy through the splendor and generosity of his light. And this joy emerges in the way in which he is sung about. Finally, "Brother Sun" fascinates; he puts things into relation with the All Powerful: "Of you, Most High, he is the symbol."

Each cosmic element is thus dreamed of in a determined sense. Water, wind, and fire, as we know, can be violent and destructive elements, but for Francis they are uniquely fraternal, benevolent, and luminous beings. Moreover, he recognizes qualities in them that are taken from no positive observation whatever and that have no objective meaning. Thus "Sister Water" is said to be "humble and chaste." These adjectives do not describe anything objective. The element is imagined, dreamed of in depth. It encloses a secret life.

In the same way, "Brother Fire" also becomes a living presence. "Beautiful, joyous, robust, and strong," he is the expression of an intimate enchantment, a reverie of fire. We know that Francis liked to sit before a wood fire during the long evenings of fall and winter, and there, for hours at a time, in a religious silence, he contemplated with wonder this companion of light, this joyous juggler, given over to all kinds of acrobatics. He let the colorful, living flame cast its subtle movement and its ardor; the two, in a sense, become one. One day Francis sat so close to the fire that his clothes caught fire but, his rapture was so great, he didn't even notice.

The things of nature of which we like to dream so much have secret links with our inward life, with our deep affectivity. We feel them as we feel ourselves. They are mirrors of our hidden energies, the symbolic language of our primal emotional forces. Dreams open the profound avenues of the soul.

Take a really simple example: a house, for instance. The house of which we dream, of which every person dreams at some point, is not merely a building of brick or wood. It is a place where living is good, where we find calm, intimacy, and warmth. It is a nest woven of intimate values. This calm and secure house in which the dreamer likes to imagine himself happy is a maternal symbol. This dream house is the language of deep emotion; it sends us back to an original experience of communion with life. Psychologists have studied drawings of houses done by young children, and one has noted: "To ask a child to draw a house is to ask him to reveal the deepest dream in which he wants to shelter his happiness; if he is happy, he will be able to find a protected house, a house both solid and deeply rooted. It is drawn in its shape, but almost always some trait designates an interior strength. In some drawings, apprarently, it is warm inside; there is a fire, a fire so lively that it can be seen jumping out of the chimney. When the house is happy, the smoke gently plays over the roof."

We can say the same for water, wind, fire, and the earth. All these elements, insofar as they are dreamed and insofar as they fascinate us, are the language of this primal affectivity. The thing of which we dream expresses at one and the same time both the world and ourselves. More precisely, it expresses our being-in-the-world in its primal strengths of adhesion to and communication with life.

When we come to the world of things dreamed, we are therefore dealing with the most obscure part of ourselves, the best and the worst, with all the forces of desire. In all times and in all civilizations men have expressed their most primitive desires, as well as their highest spiritual experiences, in a symbolic way in terms of cosmic realities: by both celebrating them and dreaming them. The history of myths and religions shows us that the sun, the moon, water, wind, fire, earth, etc., are great symbols, evoking fascinating and redoubtable forces, forces both cosmic and intimate, the bearers of life and of death.

Water, for example, has been a powerful emotional symbol for millennia. We find it as often in poetry, painting, songs, legends, and dreams as in the most evolved religious symbolism. Water is a maternal symbol, and a dream about water returns man to the source of life, to the maternal womb, to the beginning of the world, to the abyss of primordial and fecund waters. Water is a symbol of life and rebirth, but it can also be a symbol of death. Water engulfs the person who gives himself over to it passively. A "water dream" thus expresses a return to the primal sleep, a dissolution in the elementary. Like all great symbols, water is an ambivalent power.

The same is true for "our mother the Earth," explicitly sung about by Francis as a maternal symbol, and for all the other elements.

If we admit this cryptic and symbolic dimension of the cosmic elements in their religious and poetic celebration, we begin to sense the profound meaning of the Canticle of Creatures. But not only are the elements dreamed of here; their very ordering, which forms the structure of the song, is also connected with the dream. The different cosmic elements are not, in fact, evoked here in a random and unordered way but in a regular alternating of fraternal sororal pairs. Thus we have a series of three pairs: Brother Sun and Sister Moon, Brother Wind and Sister Water, Brother Fire and Sister our mother the Earth. The pair Sun-Earth frames the whole. Such an ordering has no objective meaning. Nor does it have any correspondence with the cosmological theory of the four elements that was current in that era. On the contrary, it has numerous correspondences in the history of myths and religious symbolism. Its explanatory framework is that of the great dream images in which the original forces of the human soul have been expressed since all time.

It is in this light that we should now try to understand Francis' canticle and bring out its hidden meaning. Under cover of a celebration of the world, Francis is dealing with himself, with his own depths. By dreaming of the "precious" and "fraternal" substance of things he fraternizes with the fascinating and redoubtable depths of the human soul. Unconsciously, of course, but in a real way. Like Pierre Emmanuel's shepherds, he probes "the heights of heaven in his soul, and his soul beyond that." These great cosmic images—Brother Sun, Sister Moon, Brother Wind, Sister Water, Brother Fire, Sister our mother the Earth— all express a fraternal communion not only with natural realities but also with the intimate forces that work in the human soul, that constitute our "archaelogy." The fraternity expressed in this canticle reaches out not only to the material elements but to all that the latter, duly valorized in dreaming, symbolize about the depths of the soul.

Francis opened himself to creatures in wonder and tenderness. And they, in return, opened him to himself, to the wholeness of man and his mystery.

We begin to sense a great experience for which the Canticle of Creatures would be the symbolic language. What is the nature of this experience? We would now like to respond to this question.

6
The Tamed Wolf

What inner experience is on its way to the light of
day here? The great cosmic symbols put man in relation with the obscure and fascinating forces of his
being. But what happens once this contact is made? It
is not enough to get in touch with one's depths to be
saved. Many have entered the shadowy cave hoping
to see a precious treasure shining there and have been
devoured by the dragon. The road into the depths is
always a dangerous road. This is why the "reasonable"
man is afraid of it and avoids it. But this is also the
road of life and progress. It leads to an abyss or to
a summit. "According to the way one goes into it,"
wrote Teilhard de Chardin, "a whirlwind bears one
into the shadowy depths or lifts one up onto the
azure of the heavens."

We should pay closest attention to the manner in
which the different cosmic elements are seen and felt
by St. Francis. The great images, at once ancestral,
fascinating, and redoubtable, like "Lord Sun" or

"our mother the Earth", present a fraternal visage in this canticle. The man who fraternizes with them like this does not feel dominated by them; he is not crushed by the obscure forces they represent and symbolize. No anguish casts its shadow here. No trace of agressivity appears. The elements are stripped of their destructive character. Serenity and light reign from one end of the canticle to the other. Each cosmic image is bathed in this peaceful atmosphere. The serenity is such that one could easily be mistaken and miss the depth of the canticle, seeing only the expression of a candid and naive vision of the world.

This first discovery leads us to think that the profound experience, which here reaches language, is an experience of reconciliation. This great serenity, which, we should not forget, came at the end of a whole life, is the sign of an interior calm, a deep acceptance of self, a reconciliation between the highest part of man and the instinctive and affective forces that work obscurely within him. The primal forces of desire, those great life and death forces, have lost their troubling and menacing side here. Francis no longer had anything to fear from these wild forces. He did not destroy them; he tamed them, as he tamed the wolf of Gubbio. Isn't this wolf precisely the symbol of the agressivity that can destroy us but can also become a force of love? For Francis, this primal energy had become fraternal; it was integrated with the impulse of all his being toward the Most High. Isn't it this energy that sings in the images of Brother Fire, "beautiful, joyous, unconquerable, and strong," and of Brother Wind who reinvigorates every creature with his powerful breath? The language of the Canticle of Creatures would thus be that of a "poetics" of the reconciliation of man with his inner "archaeology."

But we can go further in the exploration of this experience. As a matter of fact, a second item draws

our attention in the canticle. Francis not only celebrates creatures that manifest strength and exuberance,
such as the sun, wind, and fire; he also sings of
those that lead him to dream of a life both secret and
fecund, such as water and earth. His canticle is com-
posed of an alternating series of masculine images and
feminine images. The two sides of the human soul,
animus and *anima,* move hand in hand here like brother
and sister. To an element dreamed of in terms of
strength and action corresponds an element dreamed of
in terms of intimacy and depth. Thus alongside
"Milord Brother Sun", who shines forth in great
splendor with immense joy, are set the luminous
sisters of the night, "clear, precious, and beautiful."
In the same way, alongside Brother Wind, who un-
furls and blows freely, is Sister Water, "humble,
precious, and virginal." And Francis fraternizes at the
same time with the cosmic vigor of the first and with
the secret life and receptive depth of the second. Finally, alongside Brother Fire, the joyous and muscled
juggler, is set Sister maternal Earth, who bears and
nourishes us. Francis unites in one and the same
fraternal love the impetuous vitality of the flame and
the fecund patience of ancestral earth.

This alteration reveals a soul open to all its powers:
not only to the rational powers of action and conquest but also to the instinctive and affective powers of
receptivity and communion. The man who sings here
of all creatures is not a man identified with his rational *logos* and his ability to dominate; he is not content
merely to organize things, to do "useful" work, to
make his mark on the world according to some criter-
ion of efficiency. He is, also, a man who takes care
not to lose contact with a deeper world: a world of
inner values that belong not to the domain of doing
but to that of being. In short, a man who is open to
the secret of being and its gratuity.

The Canticle of Creatures appears to us more and more as the language of a man who is reconciled with his affective whole, who is born to a new and complete personality. A third observation will lead us to the very heart of that new personality. In the Canticle of the Sun it is impossible to separate communion with creatures from the impulse toward the Most High. By fraternizing with creatures and with all they symbolize of unconscious forces, Francis opens himself to the primitive breath of being and of life: to creative love itself. This is to say the he undoubtedly reaches to God with all the soul, with all the obscure forces of life and of desire. His spiritual life is built with these forces. *With,* and not *over against* or *alongside* or *above.* All dualism is overcome. The split between life and spirit is ended. The living forces participate in the highest destiny of the person. It is they who are singing in the light of Brother Sun, in the brilliance of Sister Moon and the Stars, in the limpidity of Sister Water, in the ardor of Brother Fire. They have ceased being obscured, entirely.

We are in the presence of a rather rare case of the spiritualization of life and the vivification of spirit. Here there is no longer a spiritual life on one side and a simply natural life on the other. There is not, on the one hand, spirit, with its noble aspirations, and, on the other, a subterranean life, with its hidden desires and impulses . All this is finally unified. We are not, to be sure, dismissing the severe and sometimes inhuman struggle that Francis waged against his own body, against what he familiarly referred to as ''Brother Ass'' and from which he had the grace to ask forgiveness at the end of his life. But there is something remarkable here: the strictest asceticism did not alter the primal forces of communion with life in Francis. His capacity for wonder, his tenderness, and his lyricism remained intact. Nothing of what

made up his living personality was stifled. It sometimes happens that an intense and badly oriented
spiritual development works itself out in a distrust or
aggressivity toward whatever links man to nature:
toward man's affective and instinctive powers. This
did not happen with Francis. Louis Lavelle correctly
writes: "There has perhaps never been a consciousness
more open than that of Saint Francis, a sensitivity
more spontaneous, more delicate, or more briskly shak-
en by all the touches he received from nature, from
other persons, and from God."

The profound originality of Francis's personality comes
from the fact that it reconciled, in a concrete and
living way, things that are apparently irreconcilable. It
reunited purity of spirit and lyricism of life, love of
the cross and celebration of the sun, identification with
the crucified Christ and affective communion with
nature. His canticle is the song of a person in whom
night and its torments are transfigured into light.

There is an episode in the life of St. Francis that
illustrates this transfiguration of the person in a symbolic way. The event happened at the beginning of
the Franciscan fraternity when, Francis was absent
and the little community of brothers was on its own.
"And behold, about midnight, when some of the
brothers were resting and some were praying in silence
with great devotion, a most splendid fiery chariot
entered through the door of the house; a huge globe
of light rested above it, much like the sun, and it
lit up the night. The watchers were dazed, and those
who had been asleep woke up and were frightened;
and they felt no less a lighting up of the heart than
a lighting up of the body. Gathering together, they
begain to ask one another what it was; but by the
strength and grace of that great light each one's con-
science was revealed to the others. Finally they understood and knew that it was the soul of their holy

father that was shining with such great brilliance."[1]

The brothers did not hestitate to recognize the soul of Francis in the fiery chariot. The image of the solar chariot is one of those basic images whose meaning concerns the human vocation in whatever is essential. The chariot, horse drawn and bearing the sun, symbolizes a whole in which animal nature and its wild forces are found associated with the luminous and divine element. This image is a symbol of the reconciliation of spirit and life, of our divine destiny and our inner "archaeology." We should not be surprised, then, if this image is often associated with an ascension to heaven: the hero, transformed into a sun, is carred off in the air on a fiery chariot. So it is with Elijah in the Bible. And so it is with Francis himself in the fresco Giotto consecrated to this episode in his life.

Nothing can better illustrate the profound experience of reconciliation expressed in the Canticle of Creatures than this nocturnal passage and this marvelous midnight sun.

7

Beneath the Sign of Forgiveness

Something would be missing from the Canticle of Creatures if God had not been praised by the most noble creature of all: man himself. This cosmic praise, it is true, is already full of human presence, as we have demonstrated, but the next-to-last stanza is explicitly consecrated to the praise of the merciful and peaceful man.

> Praised be you, my Lord, for those
> who forgive out of love for you;
> who bear trials and sickness;
> happy are they if they endure in peace:
> by you, Most High, they will be crowned.

This couplet was not part of the original canticle. It was added by Francis when he sent his brothers to sing it before the bishop and the *podestà* of Assisi, to bring these two men to a reconciliation. Even so, do we have to think of this as a circumstantial addition with no deep relation to the rest of the work?

41

At first glance, the stanza is out of step with the rest of the canticle. It takes us into another world; or so it seems. The cosmic praise of the rest of the hymn unfolds entirely under the sign of an unblemished fraternity. Yet here we are plunged into a world where tension, conflict, and suffering appear, where man is confronted with others like himself and with sickness and all sorts of trials as well.

And yet Francis wanted to incorporate this stanza into his canticle of light. By thus extending cosmic praise with that of the man of forgiveness and peace, not only did he complete his work, he revealed its profound meaning. This stanza, which first of all seems tailor made for an outside circumstance, is in reality the blossoming of the fundamental inspiration of the canticle. The latter truly appears as the song of the man reconciled, merciful, sunlike, in the image of the Most High.

To understand the sense of this couplet we have to see in it the expression of a personal experience of Francis and link it to Francis' relational life. We would miss the point entirely if we thought that this life of relations with others fell completely under the sign of universal fraternity. Francis *became* the universal brother; he was not such in the beginning. How did he open his universe to everyone? How did he discover the secret of mercy and peace? This is the question that concerns us most.

Francis was not a man who ran from human contact. On the contrary, this merchant's son was naturally open to exchange with others. Endowed, moreover, with a very rich affective nature, young Francis loved company. Contact with others was easy and pleasant for him; he easily entered into sympathy with others. "Gentleness, charm, patience, more-than-human affability, a generosity going even beyond his resources"[1] —all traits, according to St. Bonaventure, that distinguished the young Francis when he was still in the world.

All this natural affective richness was heightened by contact with the cultural movement of that era. Francis' youth unfolded in a context of civilization that was characterized by the appearance and diffusion of the ideal of courtly love. Arising from the seignorial courts of southern France, this ideal spread very quickly throughout Europe by means of the troubadours' songs and novels about chivalry. More than a passing fad, it provoked a real revolution in mores and sensibilities. Love was celebrated as *the* point of life. In its exaltation of woman, this love was less a carnal possession than the heart's reaching out toward a "distant" lady, a silent and veiled adoration, and an elevation of the soul in the joy of loving and being loved. The songs of the troubadours endlessly recount the desires, fears, and joys of the loving heart. This delicacy of feeling, this art of loving marked by veneration and tenderness—in a word, this "courtesy" —found a deep echo in Francis' heart. It inspired and modeled his young affective forces. For this young person, whose possibilities for loving were so great, this awakening of sensitivity in the lyric breath of courtly love was an emotion out of the depths: a wonder like that which struck the young Percival when he saw the first gleam of knight's armor in the forest. This new emotion was to accompany Francis throughout his life.

But his idealized *eros* was counterbalanced in Francis by a concern with appearances. Francis needed to be admired, to distinguish himself from others and lift himself above them. This was evident in his style of dress, which was both sumptuous and extravagant. And he flaunted a notorious prodigality. He spent foolishly, in a princely way, throwing banquets and feasts. He sought in everything to singularize himself, to be the center of all attention. And with great flair, he was successful—a real sun. Everyone hailed him as the king of the golden youth of Assisi. His ambition increased with age. Only God knows how much Francis secretly despised the occupation of his father, the fabric merchant. If he should dream of his father's shop in his sleep, he saw it transformed into a magnificent palace, resplendent with the brilliance of all kinds of weapons, as in the knightly novels. And, of course, all these weapons were gleaming for Francis himself. For him and for his knights. His ambition was to become a prince who would set the whole world talking. In short, Francis was fascinated with glory.

This desire for prestige and power should have led him to consider many ways to attain his goals. If Francis had followed this inclination, he would perhaps have become a man of power in this world. He certainly would not have been this genius of love whose capacity to awaken still lives among us.

The conversion of Francis to the gospel was essentially a renunciation of this desire for appearances and for domination. He discovered in the crucified Christ the Lord of glory. And he opened himself to this marvelous love that led the most high Son of God to choose the condition of servant in this world. From this encounter with Christ a reversal of values in Francis' life had to result. He, too, chose the condition of servant and put himself at the bottom of the social scale. The forces of communion and tenderness that were in him were given free rein from that moment. Modeled on the divine *agape,* they drove him toward those persons who, until then, had been excluded from his universe: the lepers. "The Lord himself led me among them and I had pity on them."[2]

From that moment on, Francis' human horizon was marvelously open. His love went out to all men, with no distinction of class, race, or religion. It ranged from pope to sultan, by way of brigands. This was no love of humanity in general, but love of the individual person, with his specific needs and particular value. For him, each person was the object of a unique love. This is how he behaved toward the brothers the Lord sent him. And he did not conceive of this fraternal love as unmarked by esteem and veneration. "The brothers," he wrote in the First Rule of life, "should exercise care and their good spirit in revering and honoring one another."[3] "Let them always love and honor one another."[4]

Such a love excludes every trace of superiority. It calls for human relationships based on something other than a desire for domination: "The brothers will have no power of domination over one another."[5] In truth, the community Francis dreamed of realizing with his brothers is essentially a community of friends where each person feels himself welcome, known, and esteemed. A community therefore open to all men without exception.

We should not, nonetheless, represent this love of Francis for men "as an ecstatic dream and an unending smile, but rather as a harsh suffering." If Francis reconciled many men between one another and with themselves, and if he radiated an apparently infinite light and gentleness on all the people and things around him, it was because he was fundamentally involved in an inner experience of reconciliation. Yet this experience is always difficult. Truth to tell, it is impossible for a man who is dependent solely on the resources of his own good will.

One might be surprised, in reading the *Writings* of St. Francis, at the care he took to denounce agitation and anger as an obstacle to charity in oneself and in others. Agitation and anger, in fact, are for him the unmistakable sign of a possessive attitude—an attitude that is, moreover, most often unconscious.

Francis rightly saw that at the base of the rupture between persons there is always a shrinking back on oneself, a secret desire for appropriation that makes man see everything in terms of himself: his personality, his idea, his project, or his interests. And all this often under cover of the highest ideals. ʾWhen the secret desire for appropriation is thwarted, agitation, irritation, anger, and rupture are the result. Francis rightly saw, too, that man on his own cannot overcome this desire and liberate himself from this shrinking back on himself and his own works.

But it's not enough to say that he *saw* this. He *lived* it intensely, in a decisive experience. If he speaks of agitation and anger with such lucidity and perspicacity, it is because he knew of them through his own experience. He himself was tempted by agitation and anger, and in the most insidious way: in his very work of peace itself. Having worked for many years to create a fraternal human community, for two years he knew the temptation to agitation and anger. No, the sun did not always shine on Francis' relations with his brothers. There were dark days, very dark days. And they were not only cloudy, but stormy.

In appearance, everything was going marvelously: the growth of the order rapidly surpassed everyone's wildest hopes; and the popes, one after another, manifested a particular benevolence toward the brothers. Yet at this point the sky suddenly grew dark. A deep anguish seized Francis' heart. Confronted with the doings of some of his brothers, he asked himself if the project that had been born of him really continued to develop according to the Lord's plan. He saw this project, *his* project, gravely compromised. And he fluctuated between outrage and discouragement.

We have to reread the testimonies of his first biographers about this very grave crisis that Francis underwent. ''He was filled with sorrow,'' says Thomas of

Celano, "that some had left their former works and had forgotten their earlier simplicity after they had found new things."⁶ "The saint was greatly disturbed by it both within and without, in his soul and in his body. Sometimes he even shunned the company of his brothers because he could not by reason of this temptation offer them his usual smile. He mortified himself by doing without food and by abstaining from talk. He often withdrew to the forest near the church in order to pray: there he could give free rein to his grief and pour out abundant tears in the Lord's presence, so that the Master who can do all things might condescend to send him a remedy from heaven for so great a disturbance. He was plagued by this temptation for more than two years, night and day."⁷
" 'The best brothers are put to confusion,' he sighed, 'by the words of the bad brothers. . . . They transfix me with a sharp sword and plunge it in my heart all the day long.' "⁸

In reality, Francis was afraid of failure. And he was tempted to condemn some of his brothers and to retreat into a lofty and bitter silence. And this in the name of the original ideal. This crisis, aggravated by sickness, was a decisive trial for him. God waited for him there. As he always waits wherever there are roots. Francis had been invited to a supreme purification in a deepening of his poor man's faith. He had to "let go" of his work itself, to consider it as no longer his concern but the concern of God. "Tell me, O simple and ignorant little man, why are you so distressed . . . ? Tell me, who has founded this order of friars? Is it not I? I have chosen you, a simple and unlearned man, so that both you and the others may realize that I will watch over my flock. . . . I tell you, therefore: do not be distressed."⁹ Like Abraham, Francis believed this promise. It was truly the faith of a poor man that led him to a total re-

turn of himself and his order to the hands of God
and the Church; and that, at the same time, strengthened him in peace with himself and with his brothers:
with all his brothers. A peace made of patience and
mercy.

When we speak of Francis of Assisi and try to understand him in depth, we must always return to this
faith of a poor man. A faith that nothing justified,
nothing within us or around us. A faith in the sovereign, gracious, and effective love of Christ the savior.
Only such a faith can bear man beyond all conflicts
into an already reconciled universe. It alone liberates
him from fear.

Henceforth Francis could say, out of his own un-
derstanding: "He who prefers to suffer persecution
rather than be separated from his brothers certainly
perseveres in true obedience, because he lays down his
life for his brethren."[10] The example of Christ inspired
him to a new fraternal love. And to a minister of the
order who wanted to retire into solitude, far from his
brothers, on the pretext that they were an obstacle
on his path to the Lord, Francis could write with
the authority conferred only by personal experience:

> You should consider everything that makes it difficult for you
> to love God as a special favor, even if other persons, whether
> friars or not, are responsible for it, or even if they go so far
> as to do you physical violence. . . . You must love those who
> behave like this toward you and you should want nothing else
> from them. . . . This should be of greater benefit to you than
> the solitude of a hermitage.[11]

And Francis, in this same letter, reveals to us the
depth of his soul; he lets us see clearly that his inner
universe is henceforth one of forgiveness and reconciliation:

> I should like you to prove that you love God and me, his

servant and yours, in the following way. There should be no
friar in the whole world who has fallen into sin, no matter how
far he has fallen, who will ever fail to find your forgiveness for
the asking, if he will only look into your eyes. And if he does
not ask forgiveness, you should ask him if he wants it. And if
he should appear before you again a thousand times, you should
love him more than you love me, so that you may draw him to
God.[12]

The universe of the man who has given his faith
to Christ and, even as a sinner before him, keeps
all his trust in him is a universe wholly different from
that which is observed by the majority of men. Forgiveness is the sovereign reality of this universe, a
solar reality that reveals to us the splendor of the love
of God but, at the same time, absolutely renews all
our human relationships by breathing a new spirit
into them. This is what makes us pass from a universe
full of aggressivity, impatience, harshness, and rupture to a universe of peace, openness, and communion.
"Welcome one another, therefore, as Christ has welcomed you, for the glory of God."[13]

This new presence to the world placed wholly under
the sign of reconciliation, inspired Francis' Canticle
of Brother Sun. Doesn't fraternizing with all creatures mean opting for a vision of the world where
conciliation is stronger than rupture? Isn't it opening
oneself, beyond all separation and solitude, to a
universe of communion in a great breath of forgiveness
and peace?

Such a spiritual experience touches the deepest part
of the soul. It is always chaste and veiled. It is not
known except through great symbols: in a celebration
of the world where the soul, fraternally united to all
creatures, itelf takes on the brilliant color of the
sun. The man who sings the Canticle of the Sun
after coming out of the night has become solar him-

self, merciful like the Most High He can truthfully say:

> Praised be you, my Lord, for those
> who forgive out of love for you;
> who bear trials and sickness;
> happy are they if they endure in peace:
> by you, Most High, they will be crowned.

8

The Sun and Death

It was the end of the summer of 1226. The light of the sun was softer, less blinding. The vines were turning gold. And the good smell of ripe fruit filled the gardens. A doctor from Arrezzo had come to visit Francis, whose sickness had become worse.

"What do you think of my illness? "Francis asked.

"Brother," the physician responded, "everything is going to be all right."

"Tell me the truth," Francis insisted. "What do you think? Don't be afraid to tell me."

"Brother, I'll be frank with you since you've asked: your sickness is incurable with our present medical knowledge. I think you are going to die soon, perhaps at the end of September or the beginning of October."

Then Francis, lying on his bed, stretched out his hands and exclaimed: "Welcome, my Sister Death!" And even though he suffered more than usual, he seemed to be penetrated by a new joy. Then he

said: "If it be my Lord's pleasure that I should
die soon, call Brother Angelo and Brother Leo to me
so that they can sing about my Sister Death."[1]

The two brothers came and, barely holding back
their sadness, sang the Canticle of Creatures. After-
ward, Francis added the following stanza:

> Praised be you, my Lord, for our sister bodily death,
> from whom no living man can escape.
> Woe to those who die in mortal sin!
> Happy those whom she shall find in your holy will
> for the second death can do them no harm.[2]

We should be careful not to separate this stanza
from the rest of the Canticle of the Sun. It would
lose its meaning. Sun and death: Francis considered
both of them with the same fraternal regard and
united them in the same praise. What is important
is not that he sang about our Sister Death but that
he sang about her at the same time as he sang about
Brother Sun. It is really difficult and rather rare to
fraternize with the sun and with death at the same
time. How can the man who loves the sun look death
in the face without a shiver of fear? And he who
chooses death curses the sun; he no longer believes
in life. Francis sings of death as a sister, but in doing
so he continues no less to celebrate the splendor of
the world with the same enthusiasm. And it is because he believes in the value of the person and of
life even in death that he can see something shining
beneath the somber door. On that side, too, is light.
The same light as that which was a sign for him in
the splendor of the sun.

This light does not shine for everyone. Francis
recognized this: "Woe to those who die in mortal
sin." These words might seem really somber in this
canticle of light but, they indicate the gravity of the

experience this song expresses. They reveal a base
"of austere and trembling thoughts having God, the
world, sin, judgment, time, and eternity for their
object."

Francis had meditated at some length upon death.
In his *Writings* is a pathetic page on which he evokes
the bitter death of the man who has somehow identified himself with his property and who cannot let go
of it. Property, moreover, that was very wrongly acquired. But taking off from this extreme case, Francis
generalizes and envisages the situation of every man
who faces death. "All the talent and ability, all the
learning and wisdom which he thought his own are
taken away from him."[3] No property of any sort
whatever can resist the devastation of death. In the
eyes of one for whom being is having, death is fearful
and desperate, for it takes everything from him. Such
dispossession can only seem annihilation. And mortal
sin is always, in the final analysis, possession of self
and the world at any price, which prevents man from
being born to infinite being and excludes him from a
life that is essentially a gift. This is the second death.
But to the man who has renounced this proprietary
attitude toward things and himself, death appears
differently. It is no longer the enemy. It even ceases
to be a fatality. It appears as the decisive step in a
long march toward being. It is the supreme act of
this letting go of self that gives us wholly over to the
splendor of being and life.

This is how Francis saw his own death. He did not
undergo it, he welcomed it, he integrated it into his
life. He assumed it to be a deeper insertion into the
mystery of Christ: "Keep nothing for yourselves, so
that he who has given himself wholly to you may
receive you wholly."[4] This advice, which he offered to
his brothers, Francis lived fully in the face of death.
Following the example of his Lord and Master, he

made death the expression of a total love and an
absolute trust. And this is why he hailed it as a sister, beneath whose gaze he saw everything blazing
with light. This light is the ultimate secret of life.
It is the light of *agape*.

Thomas of Celano has recounted the last days and
the last moments of St. Francis for us. The brothers
were weeping inconsolably. At that point, Francis
asked for bread, blessed the bread, and gave a small
piece to each of them; then he had the gosepls brought
to him and asked for the reading of a passage from
St. John: "On the eve of Passover, Jesus, knowing
that the hour had come to leave˙ this world to go to
his Father. . . . " He thus commemorated the Last
Supper that Jesus celebrated with his disciples.[5] This
was one of Francis' last acts. He clearly indicated
therein the meaning he wanted to give to his death:
it was a communion and not a separation.

And "to perfectly resemble the crucified Christ hang-
ing on the cross, poor, naked, and suffering,"[6] he
wanted to be laid out naked on the naked earth at
his last moments. This desire for a total stripping
away and for a humble communion with the earth
expressed the orientation of a lifetime. "The hour
finally came when, all the mysteries of Christ having
been realized in him, his soul flew into the joy of
God."[7] It was the third of October, in the evening.
Over the Portiuncula, where Francis' body lay, larks
sang in the light of the setting sun.

François Mauriac, writing about his dying mother,
once said: "It is sweet to see the light! It was to the
'sacred eye of day' that Antigone could not bear to
bid farewell. . . . In the same way, my dying mother,
watching the sky of a June afternoon through the
window, exhaled the same cry as Antigone: 'It's this
light I miss, these trees . . . ,' she sighed. Francis of
Assisi missed nothing. He did not feel he was leaving

or losing anything whatever. To be sure, for a long
time already his sick eyes did not allow him to enjoy
the light of the sun. And yet he never said farewell to
it. For him it had stopped being an exterior sight and
had become an interior presence. The light of the
sun vibrated within him; it henceforth was a part of
his being. Like Violaine in *L'Annonce faite à Marie,*
Francis could truthfully say:

> "I have lost my eyes.
> Only my soul holds on in this dying body."
>
> "Blind!
> How are you walking so straight, then?"
>
> "I listen."
>
> "What do you listen to?"
>
> "Things existing within me."

Epilogue:
The Patron Saint
of Ecologists

Man's relationship with nature is again becoming one of our foremost preoccupations . The current ecological crisis is forcing us to reconsider our attitude toward natural realities.

Thanks to the development of technique, man has acquired increasingly greater power over nature. The industrial civilization, based on this power, has exploited it to the hilt by putting it at the service of the desire for yield and profit. Today the world of nature is seen as an object against which technical man, motivated by this desire for yield and profit, directs his attacks. And nothing is supposed to resist these attacks. For isn't man in the industrial age "the master and possessor of nature"? He has believed this until now, and he undoubtedly still believes it.

Yet man is today discovering that, by treating nature as he does, he is destroying his natural milieu and, at the same time, the quality—if not the possibility—of human life. The mass media and a specialized literature have drawn attention to the heavy menace that weighs on the future of humanity, due to an uncontrolled exploitation of nature and its resources.

But there is another danger that techno-industrial civilization is forcing upon humanity and of which little is said, undoubtedly because it is less apparent and concerns our deepest being. Even so, it is no less linked to our present relationship with nature. Techno-industrial civilization understands and develops only a very narrow part of man's being, precisely that part that assures him the mastery and possession of nature, that is to say, a knowledge that calculates and plans, a reason that only dominates, a desire for enterprise, conquest, and yield. Techni-industrial civilization ignores all man's affective and instinctive life: it has no concern for our sympathetic instincts or with a kind of thinking that meditates and contemplates. The values of sensitivity, communion, gratuity, and contemplation have no place on the industrial market. They are not good for anything. They are supposed to give way to efficiency and cold calculation. A whole part of man is thus relegated to the background and tossed into the shadows: everything that deeply ties man to the totality of life and being. Yet without this part, man cannot realize himself fully; he has no access to a deep humanity or to a real spiritual life.

A reason that calculates and plans certainly has many good points in its favor. It is totally legitimate and necessary. But to the extent that it becomes exclusive or even simply preponderant, it leads to an impoverishment of man. It saps at the root of the condition that is necessary for sympathy: the direct perception of life and its value. Man, steeped in technical reason, sets himself directly over the nature he exploits and pillages. He behaves as if he has no roots in it. In point of fact, he has been uprooted.

For him, the instinctive forces of adhesion and communion no longer play any role in his relationship with nature. This relationship has become totally technical. And the powers of communion, which are present there, are neutralized.

This has inevitable repercussions on the level of human relationships and social life. More and more incapable of spontaneously sympathizing with the whole of life and of being, man in the techno-industrial age reserves his sympathies for the social group that represents and defends his interests. A social movement that is based solely on a sympathetic and benevolent attitude toward all people no longer has any chance of success in our civilization. To be sure, modern man seeks a remedy to this impoverishment in the multiplication of abstract visions of humanity. All the great modern ideologies were born of this lack of vital and affective participation. But this remedy is only a mask.

In this way techno-industrial civilization, left to its own demon, doubly dooms man: by attacking his environment and by fouling the sources of sympathy and communion that are present in his depths.

Confronted with this danger, the most lucid men and women denounce modern man's attitude toward nature. Technical progress is not seen as evil in itself, only the Promethean spirit that motivates and uses it. We are invited to become open to another inspiration. An ecology specialist, Professor Lynn White, does not hesitate to invoke the example of St. Francis of Assisi; he goes so far as to propose this saint, who loved nature, as the patron saint of ecologists. The proposal is not facetious. Until our day, the man of industrial civilization has thought only of dominating and exploiting nature; he must now learn how to fraternize with it, at the risk of perishing alongside it. And who could be a better guide on this road

than Francis of Assisi? In the present disarray, we
could profit very much by turning to his singular ac-
complishment. Without rejecting the marvelous progress
of technique, we can draw inspiration from the kind
of life of which Francis is the example.

The fraternity of St. Francis toward things and
people was neither sentimentalist nor anthropomorphist.
It was marked, first of all, by great respect: a respect
that springs from a state of communion with life and
people and from a direct perception of their value.
Francis deeply sympathized with everything that is
and everything that lives. Thus "he forbade the brothers to cut down the whole tree when they cut
wood," recounts Thomas of Celano, "so that it might
have hope of sprouting again."[1] This prohibition did
not come to him from a perspective of self-interest but
out of a respect for life that included the most humble
things. In his eyes, it was necessary before all else
to preserve life, to permit it to begin again and
sprout forth once more. This is not an isolated example
from the life of Francis; it was his usual way of
reacting. Several times the same love of life impelled
him to set captured animals free.

At the bottom of this Franciscan communion with
the life of creatures is a fundamental humility. St.
Francis was very aware of the dignity of man. And
yet he did not isolate himself in his awareness of this
dignity; he did not set himself apart, at the center
of creation. And above all he did not grasp at the
place of the Creator. He recognized himself as a
creature, wholly dependent on God. And he did not
hesitate, in this respect, to place himself among creatures. He felt at home near them, among them. In
doing so, he recognized that only God is God. It was
basically a religious awareness that led him to link
himself to the world of creatures and that opened him
to the profound meaning of the world by making him

see in all creatures brothers and sisters who are born of the same creative love.

This essential religious awareness had a marvelous effect for him: it liberated his powers of sympathy from all limitations and all burdensomeness; it restored them to their primitive freshness; it allowed them free rein, without tripping them up with some superiority complex. It is a remarkable fact that the conversion of Francis to the gospel of humility and poverty, far from choking the living springs of sympathy within him, gave them their best chance for fulfillment. For him, the world was no longer an object to be dominated or possessed; it was the splendid reality in which man is admitted to be alive and to co-operate with every living thing in creation. And the current of sympathy that united Francis to the world was so strong and so deep that it brought him to recover the great creative love that is present in all being and all life. His presence with people and things participated in the love of God for his own creation.

But at the same time that his instincts for sympathy and communion were given free rein at this deep level, without searching for it, and in an unconscious way, Francis discovered the secret of a full humanity. He came into possession of his affective wholeness. The latter, lifted from its archaism and its egocentrism, worked in the light of a universal love of being and of life. It espoused the creative design itself and was joined to the impulse of the spirit, to which it communicated warmth and life. And this is what gave Francis' personality and his Christianity itself an incomparable fullness and stunning force. This is also what finds expression in the Canticle of the Sun. A stirring tribute to the Creator, this song is also a celebration of the deep becoming of man and his birth into a full life. Celebrating life and celebrating God are the same thing here. This is the end of the juxtaposition of life and faith. Faith rediscovers the language of life and life itself is fulfilled in praise and prayer.

Even today, there are men who are able to open themselves to this inspiration and to vibrate with it— the inspiration that led Francis to see himself and to behave as a real brother of all creatures. One testimony among many is Sucksdorff's film, *La grande Aventure*. In its own way, this film is another Canticle of Creatures. What happens through the film, in effect, is a great love of nature and of life. *La grande Aventure* takes place in the mysterious world of the forest. This is the symbol of the deep and secret life of nature in which man no longer participates but believes he can dominate by killing and taking. Yet here this obscure life is linked with the world of childhood. Out of pity, some children save a young otter that is caught in a trap; they capture it and secretly care for it, feeding and taming it. All this without the knowledge of the men, who continue to kill and take. Suddenly, the children have gone over to the other side: to the side of life. They sympathize and make a pact with life against man. Thus they enter into the secret game of the "great adventure." For them, the night becomes clear; the forest becomes bright, magnified by a diffused light. *La grande Aventure* is the song of the sun, of the shadows, of reflections; it is the song of the wind in the reeds at the edge of ponds, the song of the rain and the song of silence. It is life, all of life, in the universe of the forest: a simple and grave kingdom where the struggle for life is the first preoccupation. But the cruelty of this struggle does not exclude love or tenderness—the love and tenderness that are discovered only by those who, thanks to the spirit of childhood, have made an alliance with life. Thus *La grande Aventure* becomes a poem about childhood. It is a hymn to

life under all its forms and even under its supreme
form: death.

Yet the taming of the young otter is only a step
for the children. Taming is still appropriation, possession. That is why this way of participating in the
"great adventure" does not go unmarked by worries
and nightmares. The children live in fear of losing
their otter. They are afraid that someone will take
it or that it will escape. And they can't sleep because
of these fears. When they discover, one spring morning, that the otter has in fact escaped, it is first of
all a great disappointment for them, a real consterna-
tion.

But then something decisive and marvelous happens.
Seeing a flock of cranes in the sky, the children
gaze at the flying birds for a long time. Then their
faces brighten and they smile; they have understood:
the "great adventure" never stops. This time they
have truly entered into the secret of life. "The great
adventure," one of them says, "was not finished; it
was in my heart." In a heart as vast and free as
life itself. A heart simple and poor.

The Canticle of Creatures does not leave poverty
behind. Poverty is not merely the refusal to possess
things; it is much more. Before all else, it is a desire
for universal communion, a kind of unlimited receptivity. If Francis of Assisi refused all particular at-
tachment, it was in order to be free to love all creation. "All that was taken from him," writes Lavelle,
"widened his horizon." Poverty, thus understood,
brings about a true affective self-transcendence. The
powers of sympathy and communion, instead of being
fixed on limited centers of interest, are opened to the
value of being and of life. The episode of *Sacrum
Commercium* is well known: Lady Poverty has been
received by the brothers and asks how to find their
cloister. The brothers take her up the hillside, show

her the magnificent panorama, and say to her: "Lady, here is our cloister."

This marvelous cloister, wide as the universe, is not merely a spectacle to be contemplated. It is a life in which one participates. It is the creative act itself; the peson who sympathizes with all that is and all that lives participates in it by loving people and things—all people and things.

Francis was undoubtedly tempted to retire into solitude one day and to turn away from creatures to give himself over wholly to the contemplation of God. But he understood that God is inseparable from love, that he is the Love that creates and saves, and that it is impossible to meet him except by opening one-self to this creative and saving love. He who is in-finitely above the world has also chosen to be infinitely *with* it. When Francis discovered Christmas,[2] he breathed the tenderness of God in the breath of the bull and the donkey. He saw the infant wake up; and in the look of the infant he contemplated the light of life.

The man who has experienced this has no taste in his mouth for the negative. He can no longer speak of the insignificance of things. Over the most miserable stable he sees a star shining. He knows the worth of people and things, above all the worth of those whom Christ saved by his blood. This is truly a "happy science," and the Canticle of Creatures is this science that sings. It is the highest affirmation we can make of the value of beings and life, as we have received them from the hands of God.

"Hail, Queen Wisdom! The Lord save you, with your sister, pure, holy Simplicity."[3] Simplicity should not make us forget wisdom. Nothing, however, is more simple than the Canticle of the Sun, but this song is also the ripe fruit of a long wisdom. The fruit of a right accord with the universe. An airy fruit, without weight, like the winged seeds that float on

the autumn wind, bearing in their fall a hope of
life.

Footnotes

Preface

1. 1 Celano 82, p. 297. (Translator's note: All page references are to *St. Francis of Assisi—Writings and Early Biographies: English Omnibus of the Sources for the Life of St. Francis* (Chicago: Franciscan Herald Press, 1973). Where this English version differs significantly from the French original, we rely on the text in the French edition of the *Writings (Saint Francois d' Assise: Documents* (Paris: Editions Franciscaines, 1968)).)

Chapter 1. The Birth of a Song

1. Paul Claudel, *Oeuvre poetique* (Paris: La Pleiade, 1957).

Chapter 2. A Hymn to Transcendence

1. "Eating of the tree of the knowledge of good signifies appropriating one's will to oneself and priding oneself on the good one does, although in reality it is the Lord in us who accomplishes it in words or acts. . . . The fruit of the knowledge of good is thus transformed into the fruit of the knowledge of evil" (Admonition 2). "In the love that is God, I beg all my brothers—those who preach, those who pray, those who work with their hands, clerics and lay—to strive for humility in everything, not to glory, rejoice, or pride themselves inwardly for good words and good deeds, nor even for any good which God says, does, or sometimes accomplishes in them or through them" (1 Rule, ch. 17). "All powerful, most holy, most high, and sovereign God,

sovereign good, universal good, total good, you who alone are good, would that we could render you every praise, every glory, all grace, all honor, and all blessing . . . " (Praises of the Lord, final prayer). Cf. 1 Rule, ch. 17, vv. 17-19.

2. The Praises before the Office.

3. 1 Rule, ch. 23.

4. Genesis 2:19-20.

5. Genesis 32:30.

Chapter 3. Cosmic Fraternity

1. 1 Celano 80, p. 296.

2. Legenda Major, ch. 8, p. 692.

3. 2 Celano 172, p. 500; Legenda Major, ch. 9, p. 700.

4. 1 Celano 81, p. 297.

5. Legenda Major, ch. 9, p. 698.

6. Louis Lavalle, *Quatre Saints* (Paris, 1951), p. 88.

Chapter 4. Wonder

1. 1 Celano 80, p. 296.

2. 1 Celano 81, p. 296.

3. Mirror of Perfection, ch. 118, p. 1257.

4. Fioretti, ch. 13, p. 1328.

5. 2 Celano 165, p. 495.

6. 1 Celano 115, p. 329.

7. 2 Celano 165, p. 495.

8. Robert Frost, "Stopping By Woods On A Snowy Evening," *New Hampshire* (New York: Henry Holt and Co., 1923).

Chapter 5. The Depth Dimension

1. Eloi Leclerc, *The Canticle of Creatures* (Chicago: Franciscan Herald Press, 1977).

Chapter 6. The Tamed Wolf

1. 1 Celano 47, pp. 268-269.

Chapter 7. Beneath the Sign of Forgiveness

1. Legenda Major, ch. 1, p. 626.

2. Testament, p. 67.

3. 1 Rule, ch. 7, p. 38.

4. Testament of Sienna.

5. 1 Rule, ch. 5, p. 36.

6. 1 Celano 104, p. 319.

7. Legend of Perugia, 21, pp. 997-998.

8. 2 Celano 157, p. 488.

9. Mirror of Perfection, 81, pp. 1212-1213.

10. Admonition 3, p. 80.

11. Letter 4, To a Minister, p. 110.

12. Ibid.

13. Romans 15:7.

Chapter 8. The Sun and Death

1. Cf. Mirror of Perfection, ch. 122 and 123, pp. 1262-1264.

2. Ibid., ch. 123.

3. Letter 1, To All the Faithful, p. 98.

4. Letter 3, To a Chapter, p. 106.

5. 2 Celano 217, p. 536.

6. Legenda Major, 14, p. 739.

7. 2 Celano 217, p. 536.

Epilogue: The Patron Saint of Ecologists

1. 2 Celano 165, p. 495.

2. Cf. 1 Celano 84, 85, 86, pp. 299-301.

3. The Praises of the Virtues, p. 132.